Building Productive Scrum Teams

Fostering Collaboration in Scrum Teams

By

Raziela Grey
Copyright@2023

Table of Contents

CHAPTER 1

Introduction to Scrum

Scrum is an agile framework for managing complex projects that originated in the software development industry but has since found application in various other fields. It is based on the principles of transparency, inspection, and adaptation, and it promotes iterative and incremental development.

At its core, Scrum is designed to enable teams to deliver high-quality products in a flexible and collaborative manner. It provides a structured approach to project management that allows for rapid response to changing requirements and priorities. The framework emphasizes self-organization, cross-functional teams, and continuous improvement.

Scrum operates within the broader context of Agile, which is a set of values and principles that prioritize individuals and interactions, working products, customer collaboration, and responding to change. Agile methodologies emerged as a response to the traditional waterfall approach, which often resulted in delayed delivery, limited stakeholder involvement, and inflexible processes.

In Scrum, projects are divided into time-boxed iterations called sprints. Each sprint typically lasts between one and four weeks, during which a potentially shippable product increment is developed. Sprints provide a predictable and repeatable cadence for development activities and serve as a basis for planning, coordination, and feedback.

The Scrum framework consists of several key components. First and foremost is the Product Owner, who represents the stakeholders and is responsible for maximizing the value delivered by the team. The Product Owner collaborates with the team to define and prioritize the product backlog, a dynamic list of features, enhancements, and bug fixes.

The Development Team, another essential component, is a self-organizing group of professionals responsible for delivering the product increment. The team collaborates closely, shares knowledge, and collectively owns the work. They estimate and select items from the product backlog for each sprint, and they are accountable for meeting the sprint goal.

The Scrum Master, the third key role, acts as a servant leader and facilitator for the Scrum team.

They ensure adherence to Scrum principles, remove impediments, and foster an environment conducive to collaboration and high performance. The Scrum Master also coaches the team on agile practices, promotes self-organization, and helps the organization embrace a Scrum mindset.

Scrum employs a set of events to facilitate collaboration and progress. These events include Sprint Planning, Daily Scrum, Sprint Review, and Sprint Retrospective. Sprint Planning is a collaborative session where the team defines the sprint goal and selects the product backlog items to work on. The Daily Scrum is a short, time-boxed meeting where team members synchronize their activities and identify potential obstacles. The Sprint Review is a demonstration of the product increment to stakeholders, followed by feedback and adaptation. The Sprint Retrospective is a reflection on the previous sprint to identify areas for improvement.

Scrum also relies on several artifacts to ensure transparency and enable effective decision-making. The product backlog, mentioned earlier, is a prioritized list of items that captures the requirements and desired features of the product. The sprint backlog is a subset of the product backlog, containing the items selected for the current sprint. The increment is the sum of all the product backlog items completed during a sprint, representing a potentially releasable version of the product.

Throughout the Scrum process, teams continuously inspect and adapt their practices to improve product quality, team collaboration, and overall efficiency. This iterative and incremental approach allows for flexibility and responsiveness in the face of changing requirements, reducing risks associated with traditional project management methods.

Understanding Agile and Scrum

Agile is an iterative and incremental approach to project management and software development that prioritizes flexibility, collaboration, and delivering customer value. It emerged as a response to the limitations of traditional waterfall methodologies, which often struggled to accommodate changing requirements and failed to involve stakeholders throughout the development process.

At its core, Agile is driven by a set of values and principles outlined in the Agile Manifesto.

These values emphasize individuals and interactions, working products, customer collaboration, and responding to change. Agile methodologies encourage self-organizing teams, frequent customer feedback, and continuous improvement.

Scrum is one of the most popular and widely adopted Agile frameworks. It provides a structured approach to managing complex projects by breaking them down into smaller, manageable increments called sprints. Scrum offers a set of roles, events, artifacts, and rules that guide teams in delivering high-quality products.

Benefits of Scrum

Scrum offers several benefits that contribute to its popularity and widespread adoption:

1. Flexibility: Scrum embraces change and uncertainty, allowing teams to adapt to evolving requirements and market conditions. The iterative nature of Scrum allows for regular inspection and adaptation, ensuring that the product meets the customer's needs.

2. Transparency: Scrum promotes transparency by providing clear visibility into the project's progress,

impediments, and priorities. The use of artifacts such as the product backlog and sprint backlog, along with regular ceremonies like the Daily Scrum and Sprint Review, helps foster open communication and collaboration within the team and with stakeholders.

3. Customer Satisfaction: By involving customers and stakeholders throughout the development process, Scrum ensures that their feedback is incorporated early and often. This customer-centric approach increases the likelihood of delivering a product that

aligns with their expectations, resulting in higher customer satisfaction.

4. Continuous Improvement: Scrum encourages continuous improvement through frequent retrospectives. These retrospectives provide an opportunity for the team to reflect on their processes, identify areas for improvement, and make necessary adjustments. The iterative nature of Scrum allows teams to incorporate lessons learned and apply them in subsequent sprints, leading to continuous

growth and enhanced productivity.

5. Team Collaboration and Ownership: Scrum emphasizes self-organizing, cross-functional teams that collaborate closely to deliver the product increment. This collaborative environment fosters a sense of ownership, accountability, and shared responsibility among team members. By working together, teams leverage their collective skills and knowledge, resulting in improved productivity and quality.

6. Early Value Delivery: Scrum focuses on delivering valuable product increments early and frequently. This approach enables organizations to gather feedback, validate assumptions, and make course corrections as needed. By delivering incremental value, Scrum reduces the risk of investing time and resources into a product that may not meet market demands.

7. Predictability and Time-to-Market: Scrum provides a predictable cadence of iterations, allowing teams

to plan and deliver work within fixed time frames. This predictability helps stakeholders make informed decisions, manage expectations, and plan for predictable releases. The time-boxed nature of sprints ensures that teams have a clear understanding of their capacity and can prioritize work accordingly, leading to improved time-to-market and faster delivery of value.

8. Empowered and Engaged Teams: Scrum empowers teams to self-organize and make decisions collectively, fostering a

sense of ownership and autonomy. By empowering team members to take responsibility for their work, Scrum promotes employee engagement and motivation, which in turn leads to higher quality outputs and improved job satisfaction.

9. Risk Mitigation: Scrum's iterative approach allows for early identification and mitigation of risks. By delivering working increments of the product at regular intervals, teams can identify potential issues or challenges early on and address them before they

escalate. This proactive risk management approach reduces the likelihood of costly mistakes and project failures.

10.   Scalability: While Scrum is often applied to small to medium-sized projects, it is also scalable for larger and more complex initiatives. Frameworks such as the Scrum of Scrums, Nexus, and Scaled Agile Framework (SAFe) provide guidance on scaling Scrum to multiple teams and aligning their efforts towards a common goal.

In summary, the benefits of Scrum include increased flexibility, transparency, customer satisfaction, continuous improvement, collaboration, early value delivery, predictability, empowered teams, risk mitigation, and scalability. These advantages make Scrum an attractive choice for organizations seeking to deliver high-quality products, adapt to changing requirements, and achieve business success in an Agile and customer-centric manner.

Scrum Roles and Responsibilities

Scrum defines three key roles that play distinct responsibilities within the framework:

1. Product Owner: The Product Owner is responsible for maximizing the value delivered by the Scrum team. They act as the primary point of contact for stakeholders, customers, and users. The Product Owner collaborates with stakeholders to define and prioritize the product backlog, ensuring that it reflects the needs and expectations of the users.

Their responsibilities include:

- Defining and communicating the product vision, goals, and objectives.

- Eliciting and prioritizing requirements based on stakeholder feedback, market analysis, and business value.

- Creating and maintaining a well-refined and transparent product backlog.

- Collaborating with the development team to clarify requirements and ensure a shared understanding.

- Making informed decisions about the product and its release plan.

- Ensuring that the team delivers a valuable and high-quality product increment.

2. Development Team: The Development Team consists of professionals who collaborate to deliver the product increment.

They are self-organizing, cross-functional, and responsible for converting the items from the product backlog into a potentially shippable product increment. The Development Team's responsibilities include:

- Collaborating with the Product Owner to refine and estimate the items in the product backlog.

- Selecting items from the product backlog for each sprint during sprint planning.

- Organizing and managing their work during the sprint, ensuring a sustainable pace.

- Developing and testing the product increment, adhering to the Definition of Done.

- Collaborating with stakeholders to gather feedback and validate the increment.

- Continuously improving their skills, knowledge, and processes to enhance productivity and quality.

3. Scrum Master: The Scrum Master serves as a facilitator, coach, and servant leader for the Scrum team and the organization as a whole.

- Ensuring adherence to Scrum principles, practices, and values.

- Facilitating Scrum events, such as sprint planning, daily scrum, sprint review, and sprint retrospective, to ensure their effectiveness and efficiency.

- Removing impediments that hinder the team's progress and productivity.

- Coaching and guiding the team on Agile practices, collaboration, and self-organization.

- Promoting a culture of continuous improvement and learning within the team.

- Fostering a collaborative and transparent environment, encouraging open communication and trust.

- Helping stakeholders and the organization understand

and embrace the benefits of
Scrum.

- Supporting the Product
  Owner in backlog
  management and ensuring
  its transparency.

- Facilitating conflict
  resolution and promoting a
  positive and constructive
  team dynamic.

- Shielding the team from
  external distractions and
  disruptions to maintain
  focus on sprint goals.

The Scrum Master is not a
traditional project manager or
team leader but rather a servant
leader who enables the team to

work effectively and helps create an environment that fosters self-organization, collaboration, and continuous improvement.

It is important to note that while Scrum defines specific roles, it encourages collaboration and shared responsibility within the team. The success of Scrum relies on the collective effort and commitment of all team members, irrespective of their designated roles. Collaboration, communication, and a shared understanding of the Scrum values and principles are essential for effective teamwork and the successful adoption of Scrum within an organization.

CHAPTER 2

Scrum Master Fundamentals

The Role of a Scrum Master

The role of a Scrum Master is crucial in ensuring the successful implementation of Scrum and facilitating effective collaboration within the Scrum team. The Scrum Master serves as a servant leader, helping the team understand and embrace the

Scrum framework while removing any obstacles that impede progress. Some key aspects of the Scrum Master's role:

1. Facilitator: The Scrum Master facilitates Scrum events such as sprint planning, daily scrum, sprint review, and sprint retrospective. They ensure that these meetings are productive, time-boxed, and focused on achieving their intended outcomes. The Scrum Master promotes open communication, active participation, and collaboration among team

members during these events.

2. Coach and Mentor: The Scrum Master coaches the team members on agile principles, values, and practices. They guide the team in adopting Scrum practices, such as self-organization, iterative development, and continuous improvement. The Scrum Master encourages the team to embrace an empirical mindset, emphasizing transparency, inspection, and adaptation.

3. Servant Leader: As a servant leader, the Scrum Master supports the team's needs and removes any impediments that hinder their progress. They act as a buffer between the team and external distractions, allowing the team to focus on their work. The Scrum Master facilitates the team's self-organization, empowering them to make decisions and take ownership of their work.

4. Change Agent: The Scrum Master acts as a change agent within the organization, helping stakeholders and

management understand the benefits of Scrum. They promote a culture of agility, encourage continuous improvement, and advocate for the adoption of agile practices beyond the immediate team. The Scrum Master facilitates organizational change by addressing resistance, promoting collaboration, and fostering a learning environment.

5. Facilitator of Collaboration: The Scrum Master promotes collaboration within the team and between the team and stakeholders. They

facilitate effective communication, encourage knowledge sharing, and foster a culture of trust and respect. The Scrum Master ensures that the team members are aligned on goals, priorities, and expectations, enabling them to work together towards a common purpose.

6. Observer and Facilitator of Team Dynamics: The Scrum Master observes team dynamics and intervenes when necessary to address conflicts or improve collaboration. They create a safe environment for open and

honest communication, encouraging constructive feedback and promoting a growth mindset. The Scrum Master helps the team to continually learn, adapt, and improve their performance.

Characteristics and Skills of a Scrum Master

To excel in the role of a Scrum Master, certain characteristics and skills are essential. These are key attributes and abilities that make a successful Scrum Master:

1. Strong Leadership: A Scrum Master should exhibit strong leadership qualities, including the ability to guide and motivate the team. They should lead by example, inspire trust, and empower team members to take ownership of their work.

2. Excellent Communication: Effective communication is vital for a Scrum Master to facilitate collaboration, resolve conflicts, and ensure a shared understanding within the team. They should be skilled in active listening, clear articulation, and

facilitating effective conversations.

3. Empathy and Emotional Intelligence: A Scrum Master should possess empathy and emotional intelligence to understand and address the needs, concerns, and motivations of individual team members. They should be able to foster a supportive and inclusive team culture, promoting psychological safety and trust.

4. Facilitation and Coaching: The ability to facilitate meetings and events, such as sprint planning and

retrospectives, is crucial for a Scrum Master. They should be skilled in creating an environment that encourages participation, engagement, and collaboration. Additionally, the Scrum Master should possess coaching skills to guide the team towards self-organization and continuous improvement.

5. Problem Solving and Conflict Resolution: A Scrum Master should be adept at problem-solving and conflict resolution. They should be able to identify and address

impediments that hinder the team's progress and facilitate effective resolution of conflicts within the team or with external stakeholders.

6. Continuous Learning and Adaptation: A Scrum Master should have a growth mindset and a passion for continuous learning. They should stay updated with industry trends, agile practices, and Scrum frameworks to continually enhance their knowledge and skills. Additionally, they should be open to feedback and adaptable to changes in the

team and organizational context.

7. Organizational Awareness: A Scrum Master should have a good understanding of the organizational dynamics and the broader context in which the team operates. This awareness helps them navigate organizational challenges, advocate for agile principles, and facilitate collaboration between the team and other stakeholders.

Building Effective Scrum Teams

Building effective Scrum teams is crucial for achieving success in agile projects. considerations for building and nurturing high-performing Scrum teams:

1. Skill Diversity: A successful Scrum team should have a diverse set of skills and expertise. Each team member brings unique capabilities and perspectives that contribute to the team's ability to deliver a quality product. The Scrum Master should ensure that the team has the necessary skills to fulfill

the product requirements and address challenges.

2. Collaboration and Trust: Collaboration and trust are foundational elements of effective Scrum teams. The Scrum Master should foster an environment where team members feel safe to express their ideas, ask for help, and challenge the status quo. Building trust within the team enhances communication, cooperation, and shared accountability.

3. Clear Roles and Responsibilities: The Scrum Master should

ensure that the roles and responsibilities of each team member are well-defined and understood. This clarity helps avoid ambiguity and confusion, allowing team members to focus on their areas of expertise. Clear roles also facilitate effective coordination and decision-making within the team.

4. Continuous Improvement: A high-performing Scrum team embraces a culture of continuous improvement. The Scrum Master should encourage the team to reflect on their processes, identify areas for

improvement, and experiment with new approaches. Regular retrospectives provide a forum for the team to learn from their experiences and adapt their practices accordingly.

5. Empowered and Self-Organizing: The Scrum Master plays a vital role in empowering the team and promoting self-organization. Empowered teams have the autonomy to make decisions and take ownership of their work. The Scrum Master should facilitate a collaborative decision-making process,

delegate responsibility, and support the team in solving problems independently.

6. Supportive Environment: The Scrum Master should create a supportive environment that fosters innovation, creativity, and psychological safety. Team members should feel encouraged to take risks, share ideas, and experiment with new approaches without fear of failure. The Scrum Master should also advocate for the team's needs, ensuring that they have the necessary resources and support from the organization.

7. Continuous Learning and Adaptation: Building an effective Scrum team requires a commitment to continuous learning and adaptation. The Scrum Master should encourage a culture of learning within the team, supporting their professional development and providing opportunities for acquiring new skills and knowledge. They should also be open to adapting team structures and processes based on feedback, changing requirements, and evolving business needs.

8. Clear Communication: Effective communication is vital for building and maintaining a cohesive Scrum team. The Scrum Master should promote clear and transparent communication channels within the team, ensuring that information flows freely and everyone is well-informed. They should facilitate effective communication between the team and stakeholders, helping to manage expectations and address any misunderstandings.

9. Celebrating Successes: Recognizing and

celebrating team achievements is essential for maintaining motivation and fostering a positive team culture. The Scrum Master should acknowledge and celebrate the team's successes, both big and small. This can be done through public recognition, team events, or simply expressing gratitude for the team's hard work and dedication.

10.   Conflict Resolution: Conflicts can arise within any team, and it is the Scrum Master's responsibility to address them promptly and

effectively. They should promote a culture of open dialogue and constructive feedback, helping team members to resolve conflicts in a healthy manner. The Scrum Master should facilitate discussions to understand the root causes of conflicts, encourage active listening, and guide the team towards finding mutually agreeable solutions. They should also mediate conflicts between the team and external stakeholders, promoting a collaborative and win-win approach.

11.   Continuous Team Evaluation: Building an effective Scrum team requires ongoing evaluation and assessment. The Scrum Master should regularly assess the team's performance, both as individuals and as a collective unit. This evaluation can include feedback sessions, performance reviews, and retrospective discussions to identify areas of improvement and address any gaps or challenges.

12.   Supportive Team Environment: A supportive team environment is crucial

for fostering collaboration, creativity, and a sense of belonging. The Scrum Master should create an atmosphere where team members feel comfortable sharing ideas, asking questions, and taking risks. They should actively promote trust, respect, and inclusivity within the team, ensuring that everyone's contributions are valued.

13.   Agile Mindset: Finally, building an effective Scrum team requires cultivating an agile mindset within the team. The Scrum Master should encourage the team to

embrace agility, adaptability, and a focus on continuous improvement. They should promote the values and principles of Agile, such as customer collaboration, responding to change, and delivering value incrementally.

CHAPTER 3

Scrum Framework

Scrum Events

Scrum defines several key events, also known as ceremonies or meetings, that provide structure and opportunities for collaboration within the Scrum framework. These events help the Scrum team stay aligned, inspect and adapt their work, and deliver value incrementally.

Sprint Planning

Sprint Planning is a collaborative meeting held at the beginning of each sprint, where the Scrum team plans the work to be completed during the upcoming sprint. The key objectives of Sprint Planning include defining the sprint goal, selecting the items from the product backlog to be worked on, and creating a sprint backlog. Here's an overview of Sprint Planning:

- Part 1: The Product Owner discusses the prioritized product backlog items with the Development Team, clarifying the requirements, and answering any questions.

- Part 2: The Development Team determines how

many items they can commit to delivering during the sprint based on their capacity and velocity. They decompose the selected product backlog items into smaller, actionable tasks.

- The outcome of Sprint Planning is a well-defined sprint goal, a set of selected product backlog items turned into tasks, and a shared understanding among the team regarding the scope and expectations for the sprint.

Daily Scrum

The Daily Scrum, also known as the daily stand-up, is a short and time-boxed meeting held every day during the sprint. It provides an opportunity for the Development Team to synchronize their efforts, discuss progress, and plan their work for the day. The Daily Scrum include:

- Time and Duration: The Daily Scrum is typically held at the same time and place every day and should be time-boxed to 15 minutes or less to ensure focus and efficiency.

- Attendees: The Daily Scrum is attended by the members of the Development Team, including the Scrum Master. The Product Owner may also attend but primarily as an observer.

- Three Questions: Each Development Team member answers three questions during the Daily Scrum:

    1. What did I accomplish since the last Daily Scrum?

    2. What will I work on until the next Daily Scrum?

    3. Are there any impediments or

challenges blocking
my progress?

- Focus on Collaboration:
  The Daily Scrum fosters
  collaboration and
  transparency within the
  Development Team. It
  allows team members to
  identify dependencies,
  provide updates, and
  coordinate their efforts.

- Impediment Resolution: If
  any impediments or issues
  are raised during the Daily
  Scrum, the Scrum Master
  facilitates their resolution
  by removing obstacles or
  escalating them to the
  appropriate channels.

- Adjustments and Planning: Based on the discussions in the Daily Scrum, the Development Team may make adjustments to their plans, update their tasks, or seek help from other team members.

The Daily Scrum is not meant to be a detailed status update meeting but rather a time for team members to sync up, identify potential issues, and collaborate on resolving them. It helps the team maintain a clear focus and transparency throughout the sprint.

Sprint Review

The Sprint Review is a collaborative meeting held at the end of each sprint to inspect and adapt the increment and gather feedback from stakeholders. The primary purpose of the Sprint Review is to demonstrate the work completed during the sprint and gather insights to inform the product backlog.

- Demo of the Increment: The Development Team showcases the work completed during the sprint, providing a live demonstration or presentation to the stakeholders. This allows them to see the functioning increment and provide immediate feedback.

- Feedback and Discussion: Stakeholders, including the Product Owner, customers, users, and other relevant parties, are invited to provide feedback on the increment. They can ask questions, share insights, and suggest changes or improvements.

- Review of Product Backlog: The Product Owner reviews the product backlog in light of the feedback and insights gathered during the Sprint

Review. This helps in prioritizing and refining the backlog for future sprints.

- Adaptation and Next Steps: Based on the feedback and discussions, the Scrum Team, led by the Product Owner, identifies any necessary adjustments or changes to the product backlog, sprint goals, or upcoming sprints.

- Collaboration and Transparency: The Sprint Review promotes collaboration and transparency between the Development Team, Product Owner, and stakeholders. It facilitates a shared understanding of the increment's value and guides the future direction of the product.

The Sprint Review is an important opportunity for the Scrum Team to gather valuable feedback, validate assumptions, and ensure that the product is on the right track. It helps the team continuously improve and refine their work based on stakeholder inputs.

Sprint Retrospective

The Sprint Retrospective is a dedicated meeting held at the end of each sprint to reflect on the team's performance, identify areas of improvement, and create a plan for implementing changes in the next sprints. The Sprint Retrospective focuses on the process, teamwork, and collaboration within the Scrum Team.

- Reflection: The Scrum Team reflects on the sprint, discussing what went well, what could have been done better, and any challenges or issues encountered during the sprint.

- Identify Improvement Opportunities: The team identifies specific areas for improvement, such as communication, processes, tools, or collaboration. This may include both positive aspects to reinforce and negative aspects to address.

- Root Cause Analysis: The team delves into the underlying causes of the identified issues or challenges to understand their origin and prevent their recurrence in future sprints.

- Action Planning: The team collaboratively creates a plan for implementing the identified improvements in the next sprint. This may involve setting actionable goals, defining new processes, adjusting existing practices, or experimenting with different approaches.

- Ownership and Accountability: The Scrum Team takes ownership of the identified improvements and commits to implementing them in the upcoming sprints. Each team member may take on specific responsibilities to drive the changes forward.

- Continuous Improvement: The Sprint Retrospective reinforces the mindset of continuous improvement within the Scrum Team. It encourages reflection, adaptation, and learning from experiences to enhance team effectiveness and delivery.

- Inspect and Adapt: The Sprint Retrospective is an opportunity for the team to inspect their own performance and adapt their processes accordingly. It helps the team become more self-aware, resilient, and efficient in delivering value.

The Sprint Retrospective is a valuable practice for fostering a culture of learning and continuous improvement within the Scrum Team. It encourages open and honest communication, builds trust among team members, and promotes a sense of collective ownership and accountability for the team's success.

Scrum Artifacts

Scrum defines three key artifacts, which are tangible work products or information radiators that provide transparency, visibility, and guidance for the Scrum Team and stakeholders. These artifacts serve as a foundation for collaboration, planning, and decision-making.

Product Backlog

The Product Backlog is an ordered list of all the desired features, enhancements, and fixes for a product. It represents the requirements and expectations from the stakeholders and serves as the single source of truth for the Scrum Team regarding the work to be done.

- Product Vision: The Product Backlog is aligned with the product vision and represents the roadmap for achieving the desired product outcomes.

- User Stories and Items: The Product Backlog consists of user stories, epics, or any other granular items that capture the product requirements from the perspective of the users or customers.

- Prioritization: The Product Backlog is ordered based on the value and importance of the items. The Product Owner is responsible for continuously refining and prioritizing the backlog, ensuring that the most valuable items are at the top.

- Emergent Nature: The Product Backlog is dynamic and evolves over time as new insights, feedback, and changes in market conditions emerge. It allows for flexibility and adaptability in responding to evolving needs and priorities.

The Product Backlog serves as a communication tool between the Product Owner and the Scrum Team, guiding their work and providing clarity on what needs to be delivered.

Sprint Backlog

The Sprint Backlog is a subset of the Product Backlog, containing the selected items that the Development Team commits to delivering within the current sprint. It represents the plan for accomplishing the sprint goal and serves as a tactical guide for the Development Team. Here's an overview of the Sprint Backlog:

- Selected Product Backlog Items: The Sprint Backlog includes the specific product backlog items that the Development Team has committed to completing during the sprint. These items are broken down into smaller tasks or user stories.

- Task Decomposition: The Development Team collaboratively decomposes the selected items into actionable tasks, estimating effort and defining the necessary work to complete each task.

- Daily Progress Tracking: The Sprint Backlog is used by the Development Team to track their progress, update task statuses, and ensure that they are on track to achieve the sprint goal.

- Self-Organization: The Development Team is responsible for managing the Sprint Backlog, including task assignments, effort estimation, and task completion. They determine how the work will be done and self-organize to achieve the sprint goal.

The Sprint Backlog provides transparency into the Development Team's work during the sprint and facilitates a shared understanding of the progress and remaining work.

Increment

The Increment is the sum of all the completed and potentially releasable product backlog items at the end of a sprint. It represents the tangible outcome of the team's work and should be in a usable state. Here's an overview of the Increment:

- Definition of Done: The Definition of Done is a shared agreement within the Scrum Team regarding the quality criteria that need to be met for a product backlog item to be considered complete and potentially releasable. It ensures that the Increment meets the necessary standards and is of value to the stakeholders.

- Incremental Delivery: The Scrum Team aims to deliver a potentially shippable increment at the end of each sprint. This means that the work completed during the sprint is in a state that could be released to the users or customers, even if the decision to release is not made.

- Feedback and Validation: The Increment provides an opportunity for stakeholders to provide feedback and validate the work done by the team. This feedback informs future iterations and helps in adjusting the product backlog and priorities.

- Transparency and Visibility: The Increment provides visibility into the progress and value delivered by the Scrum Team. It allows stakeholders to assess the product's state and make informed decisions.

The Increment represents a tangible measure of progress and value creation in Scrum. It demonstrates the team's ability to consistently deliver high-quality increments and reinforces the iterative and incremental nature of the Scrum framework.

CHAPTER 4

Coaching Agile Teams

Coaching Agile Teams is a critical aspect of being a Scrum Master and involves guiding and supporting the Development Team and the entire Scrum Team in their adoption of Agile principles and practices. The Scrum Master acts as a coach, helping individuals and teams enhance their performance, collaboration, and self-organization

- Understanding the Agile Mindset: The Scrum Master helps team members embrace the Agile mindset, which values collaboration, adaptability, and continuous improvement. They facilitate discussions on Agile principles and values, enabling team members to understand and internalize the mindset necessary for Agile success.

- Creating a Learning Environment: The Scrum Master fosters a safe and supportive environment where individuals feel encouraged to experiment, learn from failures, and share their knowledge and insights. They promote a culture of continuous learning and improvement within the team.

- Facilitating Agile Practices: The Scrum Master assists the team in understanding and implementing Agile practices such as user story mapping, iterative development, and frequent feedback cycles. They guide the team through the adoption and adaptation of Agile techniques, ensuring they align with the team's specific needs and context.

- Empowering Self-Organization: The Scrum Master supports the

Development Team in becoming self-organizing and autonomous. They encourage team members to take ownership of their work, make decisions collaboratively, and manage their own processes effectively. The Scrum Master serves as a facilitator and coach, empowering the team to find their own solutions.

- Coaching Agile Roles: The Scrum Master provides individual coaching to the Product Owner, helping them understand their responsibilities, refine their product management skills, and collaborate effectively with the team. They also support the Development Team in enhancing their technical skills, Agile practices, and teamwork dynamics.

- Conflict Resolution: The Scrum Master helps the team navigate conflicts and challenges that arise during the project. They facilitate open and constructive discussions, mediate conflicts, and encourage the use of Agile principles and techniques to address issues collaboratively.

- Continuous Feedback and Improvement: The Scrum Master encourages a culture of frequent feedback within the team. They facilitate retrospective meetings, where the team reflects on their processes and identifies areas for improvement. The Scrum Master guides the team in implementing the identified improvements, ensuring they are measurable and sustainable.

- Emotional Intelligence: A skilled Scrum Master possesses emotional intelligence and empathy, allowing them to understand team members' perspectives, motivations, and needs. They create a supportive environment where individuals feel valued, respected, and motivated to contribute their best.

- Coaching at Different Levels: The Scrum Master also coaches stakeholders and leaders on Agile principles and practices, helping them understand their roles in the Agile process and aligning their expectations with Agile values. They educate stakeholders about the benefits of Agile and support them in adapting their interactions with the Scrum Team.

Coaching Agile Teams involves guiding, supporting, and empowering individuals and teams to embrace the Agile mindset, adopt Agile practices, and continuously improve their performance and collaboration. The Scrum Master serves as a coach, facilitator, and mentor, enabling the team to navigate challenges, maximize their potential, and deliver value effectively.

CHAPTER 5

Servant Leadership in Scrum

Servant Leadership is a leadership philosophy that emphasizes the leader's role in serving and supporting the needs of others, rather than exercising traditional command and control authority. In Scrum, the Scrum Master embodies the principles of Servant Leadership, enabling the Scrum Team's success.

- Fostering a Supportive Environment: The Scrum

Master creates a supportive and safe environment for the Scrum Team to thrive. They actively listen to team members' concerns, provide guidance and support, and remove any obstacles or barriers that may impede the team's progress. The Scrum Master encourages open communication, trust, and collaboration within the team.

- Servant Leader Mindset: The Scrum Master adopts a mindset of service, putting the needs of the Scrum Team above their own. They prioritize the well-being and growth of team

members, ensuring they
have the resources, skills,
and support necessary to
succeed. The Scrum Master
leads by example,
demonstrating humility,
empathy, and a willingness
to serve.

- Facilitating Team
  Empowerment: The Scrum
  Master empowers the
  Scrum Team by enabling
  self-organization and
  autonomy. They trust the
  team's abilities and provide
  opportunities for them to
  make decisions, take
  ownership of their work,
  and drive their own
  processes. The Scrum

Master facilitates discussions and ensures that team members have a voice in shaping their work and processes.

- Removing Obstacles: The Scrum Master actively identifies and removes obstacles that hinder the Scrum Team's progress. They work closely with stakeholders to address external dependencies, resolve conflicts, and create an environment conducive to productivity. The Scrum Master advocates for the team's needs and protects them from external distractions or pressures.

- Facilitating Collaboration: The Scrum Master promotes collaboration and cross-functional teamwork within the Scrum Team. They facilitate effective communication, encourage knowledge sharing, and foster a culture of collective ownership and accountability. The Scrum Master facilitates ceremonies, such as the Daily Scrum and Sprint Review, to ensure effective collaboration and alignment.

- Coaching and Mentoring: The Scrum Master serves as a coach and mentor to the Scrum Team, supporting their professional and personal development. They provide guidance on Agile practices, facilitate learning opportunities, and encourage continuous improvement. The Scrum Master helps team members unlock their potential, overcome challenges, and grow as individuals and as a team.

- Leading by Influence: The Scrum Master leads through influence rather than authority. They inspire and motivate the Scrum Team by aligning their

actions and decisions with
Agile values and principles.
The Scrum Master
facilitates consensus-
building, encourages
diverse perspectives, and
helps the team make
informed decisions.

- Continuous Learning and
  Adaptation: The Scrum
  Master embraces a mindset
  of continuous learning and
  improvement. They stay up
  to date with Agile practices,
  seek opportunities for their
  own professional
  development, and bring
  new insights and techniques
  to the team. The Scrum
  Master encourages the

Scrum Team to experiment, learn from failures, and adapt their processes based on feedback and insights.

Servant Leadership in Scrum emphasizes the Scrum Master's role as a servant to the Scrum Team, enabling their success by creating a supportive environment, removing obstacles, and facilitating collaboration and growth. It empowers the team, fosters a culture of trust and accountability, and drives continuous improvement.

CHAPTER 6

Removing Impediments and Fostering Collaboration

As a Scrum Master, one of the key responsibilities is to identify and remove impediments that hinder the Scrum Team's progress. Additionally, fostering collaboration among team members and stakeholders is crucial for successful Agile delivery. Some key points in removing impediments and fostering collaboration:

- Identifying Impediments: The Scrum Master actively identifies any obstacles or challenges that hinder the Scrum Team's productivity and progress. These impediments can be anything that blocks the team's ability to deliver value, such as organizational bureaucracy, lack of resources, conflicting priorities, or communication breakdowns. The Scrum Master remains vigilant and observant, actively seeking feedback from the team and stakeholders to uncover impediments.

- Prioritizing and Resolving Impediments: Once impediments are identified, the Scrum Master works with the Scrum Team and stakeholders to prioritize and resolve them. This involves understanding the impact of each impediment on the team's ability to deliver value and collaborating with the necessary individuals or departments to find solutions. The Scrum Master may facilitate discussions, mediate conflicts, and engage in problem-solving techniques to address and eliminate impediments.

- Facilitating Communication and Collaboration: The Scrum Master plays a crucial role in fostering effective communication and collaboration within the Scrum Team and with external stakeholders. They encourage open and transparent communication, ensuring that information flows freely between team members and that everyone is aligned on goals, priorities, and progress. The Scrum Master may organize and facilitate meetings, such as the Daily

Scrum, Sprint Planning, and Sprint Review, to promote collaboration, shared understanding, and decision-making.

- Building Relationships: The Scrum Master actively builds relationships with stakeholders and other teams within the organization to facilitate collaboration and overcome any potential barriers. They establish lines of communication, seek common goals, and promote a sense of shared responsibility for the success of the project. The Scrum Master acts as a bridge between the Scrum Team and the broader organization, advocating for the team's needs and ensuring alignment with organizational objectives.

- Promoting Cross-Functional Collaboration: The Scrum Master encourages cross-functional collaboration within the Scrum Team, fostering an environment where team members with different skills and expertise work together seamlessly. They facilitate knowledge sharing, encourage pair programming or collective code ownership, and create opportunities for cross-training and skill development. The Scrum Master promotes a culture of collaboration, where team members appreciate and respect each other's contributions.

- Continuous Improvement: Removing impediments and fostering collaboration are ongoing activities that contribute to the team's continuous improvement. The Scrum Master encourages the Scrum

Team to reflect on their processes and interactions during the Sprint Retrospective and identify areas for improvement. They facilitate discussions on how to enhance collaboration, address recurring impediments, and implement changes that positively impact the team's performance and productivity.

- Agile Coaching: Removing impediments and fostering collaboration often requires coaching and guidance from the Scrum Master. They coach the Scrum Team and stakeholders on

Agile principles, practices, and values, helping them understand how these concepts can support effective collaboration and problem-solving. The Scrum Master acts as a facilitator, providing insights, tools, and techniques that empower the team to address impediments and foster collaboration independently.

By proactively removing impediments and fostering collaboration, the Scrum Master enables the Scrum Team to work in a productive and collaborative environment. They ensure that the team can focus on delivering value and help create a culture of continuous improvement and innovation within the organization.

CHAPTER 7

Leading Agile Change in the Organization

As a Scrum Master, you may find yourself leading the Agile change initiative within your organization. This involves driving the adoption of Agile principles, practices, and mindset across teams and departments. Some key considerations for leading Agile change:

1. Understand the Current State: Gain a deep understanding of the current organizational

culture, processes, and challenges. Assess the readiness of the organization for Agile adoption and identify the areas that require improvement or change. This may involve conducting assessments, surveys, or interviews with stakeholders.

2. Create a Compelling Vision: Develop a clear and compelling vision of what Agile can bring to the organization. Articulate the benefits, such as increased customer satisfaction, faster time to market, improved collaboration, and

adaptability to changing market conditions. Align the vision with the organization's strategic goals and emphasize the value Agile can deliver.

3. Educate and Create Awareness: Agile change requires a shared understanding among stakeholders. Conduct training sessions, workshops, and awareness programs to educate employees about Agile principles, values, and practices. Use real-life examples and case studies to demonstrate the positive

impact of Agile in similar organizations or industries.

4. Identify Agile Champions: Identify individuals or teams who are enthusiastic about Agile and can serve as change agents or champions within the organization. These individuals can help drive Agile adoption, provide coaching and mentorship, and share their experiences and successes with others.

5. Establish Agile Communities of Practice: Create communities of practice or forums where Agile practitioners can

share knowledge, discuss challenges, and exchange best practices. These communities provide a platform for continuous learning, support, and collaboration among individuals interested in Agile.

6. Provide Coaching and Support: As a Scrum Master, you play a crucial role in coaching teams and individuals on Agile practices and mindset. Offer guidance, support, and mentorship to teams during their Agile journey. Address any resistance or challenges that arise and

help teams overcome obstacles to successful Agile adoption.

7. Lead by Example: Model Agile behaviors and values in your own work and interactions. Demonstrate transparency, collaboration, and continuous improvement. Show the benefits of Agile through tangible results and showcase success stories to inspire others.

8. Measure and Communicate Progress: Define key metrics and indicators to measure the progress of Agile adoption. Track

improvements in areas such as cycle time, customer satisfaction, productivity, and quality. Regularly communicate these metrics and progress updates to stakeholders to reinforce the value of Agile and create a sense of achievement.

9. Adapt and Iterate: Agile change is an iterative process. Continuously gather feedback, adapt your approach, and iterate on the implementation based on lessons learned. Remain flexible and open to adjusting strategies and practices to fit the unique

needs and context of the organization.

Leading Agile change requires strong leadership, effective communication, and perseverance. By creating a compelling vision, providing education and support, fostering Agile communities, and leading by example, you can drive successful Agile adoption and transformation within your organization.